# The Stranger Side of Street Art

## Unusual Graffiti and Its Stories

# Table of Contents

# Chapter 1. Introduction

Discover a world where concrete canvases burst with whispers of the unconventional, where enigmatic scrawls give voice to the silent storytellers of our streets. In our Special Report titled "The Stranger Side of Street Art: Unusual Graffiti and Its Stories", we unearth the compelling narratives often overlooked in urban landscapes, revealing spectacular beauty in the seemingly bizarre. This report isn't just paint meeting wall; it's a journey into the depths of artistic expression, swirling in the realms of the extraordinary. Inject your day with a dash of color, an ounce of inspiration, and a hefty dose of the delightfully peculiar - this isn't just a read, it's an enthralling adventure. Prepare yourself to peel back the layers of the ordinary to find piquant tales etched in the alleys of obscurity. You're just one click away from stepping into an avant-garde universe, so go ahead, buy this report; we promise it's an eye-opener into the atypical world of street art.

# Chapter 2. Unveiling the Canvas: The Birth of Street Art

Street art, in the forms of anonymous graffiti, tags, stencil work, mural painting, and wheatpaste posters, has become an integral part of city life, adorning urban landscapes with bursts of color and social commentary. However, this popular artistic medium didn't manifest overnight. The traces of its beginnings can be traced back to the dawn of human civilization.

## 2.1. Elements of Antiquity

Our journey begins in a time before cities, before rules and regulations. A time where ancient hands brought life to the cold stone walls of the caves they inhabited. Although street art is undoubtedly a modern concept, its roots stretch back many millennia. In the caves of Altamira in Spain and Lascaux in France, early humans left behind images of animals, rudimentary signs, and handprints - a poignant want for self-expression that echoes still in the graffiti-laden lanes of contemporary urban environments.

These primeval displays of art, born of charcoal, ochre, and chalk, adorn the interiors of caves like a personal testimony written in pictures. Much like modern street art, these ancient murals transcended the boundaries of language to document the human experience, to make themselves heard in a world where voices were often lost in the echoes of time.

## 2.2. Street Art in Ancient Civilizations

Moving forward in time, we find a historically documented affinity for public artistic expression in organized societies. The Ancient Greeks and Romans, for instance, had a robust tradition of graffiti. Although varied in themes, these early etchings were often personal, political, or simply entertaining. Ranging from political campaigns and declarations of love to simply lewd drawings, the graffiti of Pompeii fascinates us to date.

In parallel, across the world, the Native American Anasazi tribe practiced symbolic rock etching or petroglyphs. The Vikings, too, left behind runic inscriptions during their seafaring journeys. Remarkably, one of the graffiti found in the Hagia Sofia, Istanbul, was traced back to a Viking mercenary. These precious snapshots of times gone by illustrate that the human penchant for coding stories into stone is far from modern and is indeed imprinted deep within our collective DNA.

## 2.3. Emergence of Modern Street Art: Early 20th Century

Fast-forward to the 20th century, an era of exponential societal change, where street art began to take shape in ways that align more closely with our modern understanding of the form.

During the World War II years, soldiers would leave graffiti in combat zones, caves, or other places they passed through. The infamous 'Kilroy was Here', featuring a bald character with a long nose peeking over a wall, became one of the most proliferate pieces of street art during this era.

Closer home, the mid-20th century saw urban American cities

become hotbeds for gang-related graffiti, with city walls serving as boards declaring territorial dominion via stylized tags. The Philadelphia-based writer Cornbread, for instance, achieved nationwide recognition when he spray-painted "Cornbread Lives" on an elephant in the local zoo, demonstrating the growing audacity and recognition of street art.

## 2.4. The Boom Box Era: The 1970s and 1980s

When we think about street art today, our minds often beeline to elaborate murals and stencil-based works. Such recognizable forms were born during the late 1970s and early 1980s in places like New York City.

During this era, subway trains became the canvas of choice. 'Writers', as they were called, competed to 'bomb' as many trains as they could with their tags or 'pieces' (short for masterpieces). Noteworthy characters from this era include names like TAKI 183, a fleet footed messenger whose tag appeared throughout New York City, bringing graffiti into public consciousness.

Parallel to this, on the west coast, the Chicano Art Mural Movement gathered steam, depicting the social-political struggle of the marginalized Hispanic community. These murals form an integral chapter in the evolution of modern street art, by constituting their walls as political podiums and artistic canvases simultaneously.

## 2.5. Street Art in the Digital Age

The advent of the internet and digital media reshaped the landscape of street art once more, allowing artists to reach an international audience. Simultaneously, it also saw increased diversification in the medium and styles of street art, from stencil graffiti to sticker art, poster art, and street installations.

An exemplar of this era, the elusive Banksy, demonstrates the power of street art as a tool for social critique. Anonymous and provocative, his pieces tackle topics from war and injustice to capitalism and freedom, attracting the usual denizens and tourists alike as he continues to etch socio-political narratives onto the urban canvas around the globe.

Artists like Invader and ROA, equally iconic in their own right, further widen the spectrum of street art, demonstrating the power of gaming culture and biogeography, respectively, as sources of inspiration.

# 2.6. The Continuing Evolution

As we move further into the 21st century, the tapestry of street art continues to evolve, shaped now by advances in technology such as virtual and augmented reality, and the on-going dialogue between mainstream acceptance and its countercultural roots.

The story of street art is one of unbridled creativity, etched permanently onto the surfaces of our collective memory, embodying the rebellious, the unheard and the unconventional. It is a chronicle of artistic evolution, and a testament to the indomitable human spirit's desire for self-expression.

From the cavernous echoes of our past to the swirling vortex of our digital future, street art has been and will continue to be an integral part of our evolving cultural narrative, a constant drumbeat underlying the frenetic rhythm of life. Pulsating vibrantly on urban canvases worldwide, it awakens us to the remarkable beauty in the seemingly bizarre, driving us forth into a world that teems with possibilities - into the stranger side of everyday life.

# Chapter 3. Beyond the Tag: Unraveling the Secret Language of Graffiti

For many, graffiti is synonymous with vandalism, a destructive force that turns clean city walls into unwanted collages of chaos. Yet, for those who dare to delve beneath the surface tags and hastily sprayed monikers, there lies a rich tapestry of experiences, a secret language, and a means of communication as intricate and nuanced as any formal script. Our journey begins here, within these cryptic symbols etched onto the walls of our bustling cities, honing in on the unknown tales waiting to be unraveled.

## 3.1. A Semiotic Playground

Semiotics, the study of signs and symbols, is our primary tool in decoding graffiti's enigma. If we consider language a system of signs, then graffiti, like any other language, is composed of signs. It uses symbols, colors, and compositions to articulate a meaning that might not be immediately graspable to the untrained eye. Understanding the semiotic value of graffiti not only gives us the key to the graffiti language, but also insights into the socio-cultural context in which it was created.

Interpreting graffiti through semiotics begins with recognizing the symbols used. Tags (a graffiti artist's signature) can be seen as a personal symbol of an artist. However, they're more than mere autographs; they mark territory, represent respect, and broadcast the artist's presence. Different styles in tags could suggest variations in artist's skills and emotional state. A fluid, rounded script could signify comfort and accessibility, while jagged edges could express tension or aggression.

The choice of color, too, has semiotic importance. Dark, somber colors can express frustration or despair, contrasting with the bright colors often chosen for their eye-catching and energetic properties. However, these interpretations are not absolute; everything depends on the context, location, and individual artist.

# 3.2. Demystifying the Code

The sophistication of graffiti goes beyond the artistry of tags. Graffiti artists use a complex lexicon of terms as mix of slang and code, adding another layer of secrecy to their works. Terms such as "bombing" (covering an area with numerous pieces quickly) and "piece" (short for masterpiece, a large, detailed graffiti), indicate an inherent subculture.

Understanding these terms is the second step in delving into the graffiti's secret code. The lingo denotes more than an intention to mystify; it's also a form of protection, keeping the intentions of graffiti artists obscured from authorities and the uninitiated.

Take, for instance, the term "toy." While one might assume a playful connotation, in graffiti speak "toy" is an insult, referring to an amateur or unskilled artist. Conversely, being "up" equates to having high visibility, with a lot of your works seen around the city, which is a mark of prestige among graffiti artists.

# 3.3. Social Sentiments and Political Proclamations

Graffiti's underbelly often serves as a megaphone for social and political messages. Artists use the city's walls to amplify emotions, beliefs, and narratives that might otherwise remain unheard. These messages can range from outcry against social injustices to the expression of solidarity, or even political satire.

One of the most potent examples of this was seen in the 1980s New York, where subway train graffiti was more than stylized signature. Mixed into the colorful explosion of artistic prowess were powerful commentaries on social issues, critiques of President Reagan's administration, and poignant cultural statements. For those who could understand its language, graffiti was the visual newsreel, broadcasting underlying tensions of society right on its pulse-point.

# 3.4. The Allure of Anonymity

Being pseudonymous is a key part of graffiti culture, with artists often adopting a "nom de guerre". This culture of anonymity allows artists to express themselves freely, without fear of repercussion. The act of interpretation opens a pandora's box of identities, emotions, and narratives.

'Who is Banksy?' might be one of the most significant questions in contemporary street art, with the elusive British artist never officially unmasked in public. This elusive nature becomes part of the intrigue, prompting viewers and critics alike to investigate his pieces, teasing out meanings and crafting theories about the artist's true identity.

Delving into the secret language of graffiti leads us to the heart of a subculture that is more than the sum of its colorful parts. Each tag, each piece, is a thread in a tapestry of urban storytelling, waiting to be deciphered. The swift sweeps of aerosol paint that color our cities' walls are the medium for a robust and dynamic language. It's a language that challenges the norm, gives voice to the silent, and ignites conversations, transforming brick and mortar into a veritable canvas of stories. This chapter was merely an attempt to skim the surface, but the beauty of graffiti, like any language, lies in exploring its depths.

# Chapter 4. The Color of Rebellion: Political Graffiti Through Ages

From ancient Roman walls adorned with political statements to the modern concrete jungles resonating with vibrant expressions of resistance, graffiti has been an unfiltered medium of rebellion. Evoking strong sentiments through a unique and vivid palette, it challenges the societal norms, questions authority, and liberates spaces by providing a voice to the unheard.

## 4.1. A Burst of Antiquity: Graffiti's Early Strides

In the confinement of history, it's worth noting how ancient civilizations readily adopted graffiti as a revolutionary tool. Ancient Rome was a gallery of political graffiti, where fuelled by heightened social stratification and vast political rifts, citizens asserted their dissent on unassuming walls.

Messages varied widely, from satirical outtakes on politicians to raw declarations against bureaucratic injustice. Such was the case in Pompeii, where a graffiti read, 'I don't want to sell my husband, not for all the gold in the world'. An intimate outcry against a law made to curb debt by allowing creditors to sell their debtors, particularly spouses. This bitter resentment was a snapshot into an era rife with social outrage, validating the importance of graffiti as a uniting thread across classes, raising evocative protests against the oppressive ruling elite.

## 4.2. From Scribbles to Symbols: Iconic Graffiti of the Twentieth Century

Fast-forward to the 20th century. Cities transformed into battlefields of ideologies with walls morphed into weapons of resistance. Post-WWII Berlin, for instance, birthed distinct styles of graffiti that bore testament to post-war disruption and looming political division. The Berlin Wall, best known as 'The Longest Art Gallery in the World', witnessed countless instances of heart-wrenching, political art. Most striking was a mural of the leader of East Germany, Erich Honecker, kissing Soviet leader Leonid Brezhnev, deftly criticizing political rhetoric and the dubious nature of political alliances.

The 1968 student protests in Paris echoed similar rebellion. 'Be realistic, demand the impossible', a phrase scrawled on a Parisian wall, became representative of a generation demanding freedom from the shackles of structural inequalities. The graffiti weren't mere adornments; they were calls to action capturing a transformative period in French history.

## 4.3. Future Forward: Graffiti in the Digital Age

The advent of the 21st century brought potent visual narratives of dissent engraved on various global platforms. Colourful acts of rebellion took to the streets, striking chords with the ubiquitous turmoil of the era.

Banksy, a pseudonymous England-based street artist, stretched the artistic horizon in narrating political discontent. His iconic piece 'Girl with a Balloon' symbolizes the loss of innocence, invoking thoughts on war-stricken societies. 'Kissing Coppers', another powerful depiction, spotlights societal attitudes towards homosexuality, casting graffiti as a wall-to-wall platform propagating acceptance and love.

Away from the Western hemisphere, in the Middle East, the Arab Spring boomed with graffiti as young artists commandeered public spaces and brought forth the socio-political predicaments of the time. 'Spray', Egypt's renowned graffito, became a symbolic representation of this era, featuring a gas mask-clad protester encapsulating the shared experience of global civil unrest.

But the rebellion wasn't limited to walls. Digital graffiti evolved as resistance in territories where walls weren't as accessible. Artists exploited the digital sphere to reflect political narrative, teetering on the brim of cyberactivism. KATSU's drone-painted graffiti and street artist BLU's animations becoming emblematic of this new-age rebellion.

# 4.4. A Canvas of Change: Graffiti - The Defiant Spectacle

Strolling through this spectrum, one observes how graffiti has evolved, with every stroke infiltrating authoritative domains, and every color diverging from hegemonic narratives. A look at the omnipresent 'Free Hong Kong' graffiti or the 'Black Lives Matter' street mural serves to reiterate this fact.

And so it continues, this vibrant dance of subversion on the urban canvases. The story of graffiti as a rebellious art form, told and retold in dynamic hues, texts, and contexts, has come to symbolize a kind of raw and unfiltered emotion that is equaled by few other forms of expression. This art of the streets, often born amidst chaos and despair, grows into a resounding vessel of hope, painting the globe with audacious and transformative narratives.

Thus, political graffiti is not an element of disarray on city walls; it's an act of resistance etched in the annals of history, an unceasing conversation between the politics of space and the power of expression. It's the chronicle of the unvoiced, the dynamic color of rebellion.

# Chapter 5. Quiet Whispers, Loud Statements: The Socio-cultural Impact of Street Art

Street art, in its diverse, vibrant forms, isn't solely an eruption of creativity on an unadorned wall; it's a socially and culturally significant dialogue that echoes in every corner of the cities it graces. The game of shadows and splashes of color that adorn our urban landscapes carry much more than aesthetic appeal – they represent voices, identity, and a medium for social commentary.

## 5.1. The Pulse of the Streets

Studies of street art often revolve around the aesthetic value and artistry, but to truly understand these silent whispers, one must venture deeper. In doing so, we find that street art pulsates with the rhythm of the city it inhabits. It mirrors the views, problems, and sentiments of its people, serving as an open, raw journal of societal events and conditions.

Just like art forms preserved in museums, street art reflects the epoch it was created in. However, unlike enclosed art forms that are selectively displayed and accessible to specific strata of society, street art insists on inclusion and reaches out to every passerby, gathering gaze and thoughts like a magnet.

In numerous instances, street art has proven to be extraordinarily reactive to socio-political issues. For instance, when censorship or repression stifles the voices of the masses, the walls start speaking. The resulting body of work often presents subversive messages, critiques, and depiction of realities, veiling them in symbolism or humor.

# 5.2. A Social Commentary

Street artists often tackle socio-political issues as their subjects, making the cityscape their canvas. These art pieces frequently respond to societal unrest, political upheaval, or cultural shifts, giving form to an often-ignored reality; consequently challenging the status quo or pressing for change.

A perfect illustration of this phenomenon are the powerful murals painted during the civil and political riots. Art becomes a form of activism, transforming into a powerful tool of proclamation and protest. It brings urgency and light to subjects that are otherwise overlooked or suppressed, making them impossible to ignore.

Street art, in this capacity, gives a voice to the marginalized. Images sympathizing with poverty, addiction, homelessness, and the like find room on the city walls, stimulating discourse on often taboo or shunned subjects.

# 5.3. Cultural Reflections

Apart from its role as a tool for expression and social commentary, street art also holds a mirror to the culture and heritage of a place. Artists often draw inspiration from the area's history, folk tales, traditional art, and customs, reflecting a place's unique identity.

In some areas, street art is a tapestry of diaspora culture. For instance, murals depicting significant cultural symbols, traditional garb, homeland landscapes, and portraits of influential personalities from an immigrant community can serve as bridges between the old and new worlds.

Furthermore, it can also illustrate cultural evolution and amalgamation as societies become more heterogeneous. Such dynamic art pieces resonate with cultural pluralism, redefining local identity while offering a sense of belonging to the migrant populace.

# 5.4. Quest for Identity

Street art invariably becomes a quest for identity. Artists portray their individualism and unique perspective through their work. Simultaneously, they showcase the collective identity of the communities they represent.

At an individual level, tagging, one form of graffiti, is a statement of existence. A tag or signature symbolizes the mark of an artist, a declaration that 'I was here.' It is a stamp of their artistic style, philosophy, and existence.

On a wider scale, street art can serve as a collective assertion of community identity. Distinct motifs, styles, or symbolic representations can give an identity to different neighborhoods within a city, marking their unique cultural, historical, or social parallels and differences.

# 5.5. The Catalyst

Lastly, it's worth noting that street art is not a mere onlooker in societal progression; it is a catalyst too. The powerful socio-cultural undertones in these artworks can stir emotions, provoke thought, and indirectly push for change.

Inspiring murals, thought-provoking graffiti, and other street art expressions can spur a sense of community, unity, and pride among citizens. They can raise awareness about critical issues and even influence public opinion. In some cases, such representations of shared struggles and aspirations can fuel movements and acts of defiance.

In conclusion, the street art we encounter daily, in the nooks and crannies of our cities, is more than mere wall embellishment. It's the tangible manifestation of our social, cultural, and political lives. It's the quiet whisper of the streets finding form in loud statements of color and shape, a dialogue between the artists and the world, mirroring the city's heart and soul on bare walls. The graffiti we pass by is not just abstract color blots or elusive symbols; they are narratives of societies, waiting to be heard and understood.

# Chapter 6. Abstract Cartographies: Navigating Graffiti Across Continents

Street art, in its most brazen and provocative form, disrupts the normative landscape of the everyday. It is a public declaration, a sudden intrusion of personal or collective creativity that transforms the ordinary into the extraordinary, etching a signature of identity onto the vast, anonymizing panorama of urbanity. Yet, it is not merely an interruption, but rather a recalibration; a redefining of space which endows the urban with a new, often hidden, depth. One form that such artistic interventions take is the phenomenon of abstract cartographies, a strange but intriguing blending of graffiti with geographic notation and navigational symbols.

## 6.1. The Genesis of Abstract Cartographies

Abstract cartography came into being as street artists started to juxtapose, juxtapose, and conflate visual grammar laden with geographic lexicons alongside their graffiti. The city isn't just the surface for these artworks; it's the lifeblood, the theatre, and the map. Here, hearts beat in spray paint coursing through the arteries of alleyways, pulsating vibrantly, sending aesthetic waves across the concrete body politic.

The abstract part of the term stems from the fact that unlike traditional cartography, these artworks don't just depict locations in absolute terms but use abstraction to convey rich emotion, cultural history, or social commentary. They detour away from delineating physical boundaries to explore the contours of human experiences and narratives unfolding in the urban space.

# 6.2. Abstract Cartographies around the World

Over time, abstract cartographies have crept up across different continents, each carrying a distinctive cultural thumbprint, revealing the stories tied to the places they inhabit.

In the Americas, from the crumbling bricks of Detroit to the sun-soaked walls of Rio de Janeiro, street artists are using their work as satirical challenge to political authority or as poignant reflections on social inequities. The maps may show winding lines depicting immigration or gentrification routes. Razor-sharp edges of urban divisions become soft curves, blur the boundaries between the real and the imaginary.

Europe, with its rich history of religious and political revolutions, has seen abstract cartographies evolve into symbolic representations of changes over time. Here, the tapestry of the streets is punctuated with palimpsests of human triumphs and downfalls, social shifts and cultural evolution, all traced in the trails and nodes of graffiti maps.

Africa and Asia, buoyant with their robust cultural identities, present yet another canvas for abstract cartographies. They tend to capture the dialogue of tradition and modernity, revealing fluctuating cultural patterns and evocative narratives of coexistence in the face of rapid urbanization.

# 6.3. Decoding the Symbols

The task often posed to the observer of abstract cartographies is to decode the often arcane symbolism within them. Each squiggle, color choice, shape or symbol is a breadcrumb left behind by the artist, a clue for the viewer to trace their way back and retrieve the story.

Geometric shapes, for instance, could convey order amidst chaos.

Distorted lines could imply ruptures within a community. Colors could indicate everything from mood to societies' demographical elements. A blue hue could indicate calm or melancholy, while red may be symbolic of love or conflict.

## 6.4. Defining New Spaces

Abstract cartographies also serve as a way for graffiti artists to stake a claim on "invisible" or "lost" territories within the urban space. These might be socio-political borders, marginalized communities, or spaces forgotten or dismissed by mainstream society. By mapping these, artists spotlight them, pull them into the mainstream field of vision, effectively altering the dominant perception and reality of urban spaces.

## 6.5. Impact on Street Artscape

Such radical reimagining of space through abstract cartographies is having profound impacts on the street artscape. It is fostering a new breed of participatory street art, where the act of navigation itself becomes an act of creation. They invite viewers to engage, interpret, and become a part of the artwork. As such, abstract cartographies are reconceptualizing the viewer's role, seamlessly transitioning them from mere spectators to participators.

## 6.6. Conclusion

As graffiti and geographic narratives blend to create these uncanny maps adorning walls worldwide, they redefine our interaction with urban environments. Abstract cartographies are not merely arts painted on walls; they are sensorial journeys navigating the confluence of geography, creativity, and personal interpretation. They transcend physical dimensions to capture spatial emotions and complicate the functionality of maps, charting not just places but feelings, conflicts, histories, dreams, and ideas that ripple within these places.

Although abstract cartographies may appear unconventional, there is no denying their enthralling allure and the captivating tales they encode in urban canvases. Their continued evolution will undoubtedly inject exciting new dimensions into our exploration of street art and further our understanding of how art interplays with space, place, and society.

# Chapter 7. Of Shadows and Silhouettes: The Rise of Stencil Art

In the age of hasty hashtags and quickly abandoned aphorisms scrawled across an urban backdrop, it is stencil art that finds a rare permanence. Quietly resolute and unabashedly enigmatic, stencil art is a kind of transient tattoo etched onto the skin of our cities. This unique form of expression employs stencils - cardboards, metals or plastics with cutouts - while the artist applies paint or ink to produce images or text. The age-old art-form has been reinvigorated in the street art movement and commands an esteemed position due to its combination of creativity with stark social commentary.

## 7.1. Stencil Art: An Age-Old Technique Revisited

Stencil art is not a modern phenomenon. It's an ancient practice dating back to the Neolithic period. Early humans used hands as rudimentary stencils and blew pigment over them to create handprint outlines on cave walls. Fast-forwarding to the more recent past, stencil art was extensively used for commercial purposes such as labels and signage. Even soldiers in World War II left their mark with stencil art, utilities for identifying objects or territories during times of turbulence.

Today, they are tools for the modern creative activist, instrumental in sending powerful messages. Street artists have embraced this age-old technique and reimagined it, effectively repurposing it in a contemporary context that merges social consciousness with sharp and stirring visuals.

## 7.2. The Rise of Stencil Street Art

Mastering the art of stenciling is not just about achieving well-defined lines and amazing intricacy. It is invariably about the message being conveyed. The rise of this street art form connects with the desire for change against the culture of visual bombardment through advertising. Stencil artists transformed their subjects from mundane objects to social commentaries, giving visibility to unseen truths and unheard voices.

One name particularly synonymous with the proliferation of stencil art in recent history is Banksy. The anonymous England-based street artist, political activist, and film director made stencil art mainstream with his strokes of irony, satire, and politics, creating controversial pieces across the world.

## 7.3. Revolution on Walls: Stencil Art as a Voice

Street art, and by extension stencil art, has become an essential tool for delivering socio-political messages in recent decades. From Banksy's commentary on war, capitalism, and class, to the work of French artist Blek le Rat leveraging stencils for expressing issues related to immigration and urbanization, it has unarguably grown beyond just aesthetics. The simplicity and reproducibility of stencil art make it an effective medium for expressing dissent and rallying for change.

The voice of stencil art echoes loudly in times of socio-political unrest. Argentina, in its late 2001 economic crisis, saw the streets explode with stencil art expressing public dissent, giving birth to the artist group Arte Callejero. Similarly, the Arab Spring witnessed stencil art portraying protestors as heroes on town's walls. Stencil artists became the stealthy chroniclers of each cities zeitgeist.

# 7.4. The Evolution: From Sidewalks to Galleries

Not surprisingly, as stencil street art grew in popularity and impact, it began to command attention beyond urban alleys and boulevards. Today, stencil art has invaded the traditional gallery spaces too. The division between street and gallery art has become more fluid, with stencil pieces being sold at auctions for sky-high prices.

Still, many artists, like Banksy, choose the streets as their museum, turning urban sprawls into open-air galleries. The unpredictability and impermanence enhance the allure of stencil art, creating dialogues and encouraging participation in a way the white walls of a traditional gallery cannot.

# 7.5. Future Perspectives: Stencil Art in Virtual Reality

As technology advances, stencil artists have begun seeking new horizons. With virtual reality becoming increasingly accessible, artists do not just produce works for the physical public but also for the virtual public. VR now allows stencil art to become more immersive, interactive and non-permanent, stretching the limits of what public space can be.

In conclusion, stencil art, the old guard of artistic expression, has proven to be a powerful tool that continues to transform and evolve against every skyline it touches. It is a vibrant testament to human creativity, resilience, and zeal for change. Swirling in the extraordinary, stencil art fills our streets, and our hearts, with stories that need to be seen and heard - stories that remind us that art isn't just paint meeting wall, but a mirror reflecting our shared realities and aspirations.

# Chapter 8. Washed Away, Not Forgotten: Ephemeral Street Art and Its Significance

A gentle spring rain can transform a bustling street into a reflective mirror-world, highlighting the ephemeral fragility of our surroundings. This fluidity, the capricious ebb and flow of form, is especially characteristic of ephemeral street art, where creations are as transient as the clouds in the sky or the waters in a stream.

## 8.1. The Dance of Impermanence

Conventional ideas of art preserve permanence as a core tenet. Yet, in ephemeral street art, the transient nature of the creation is a deliberate, integral aspect of the work's potency. A mural painted with rain-activated dye, a sculpture crafted out of melting ice, or a sketch crudely drawn in wet concrete may exist for mere moments or hours, yet leave indelible impressions on their viewers. Artists create these ephemeral masterpieces fully aware of their unavoidable disappearance, celebrating the triumph of artistic expression over the fleeting boundaries of provisional existence.

Yet, this impermanence is more than a reflection of life's transience. It subtly acknowledges the constant evolution of cities themselves, mirroring the incessant flux of architectural facades and street life rhythms. Just as buildings rise and fall, as communities grow and change, so too does this art form, recorded in the raw echo of urban souls.

## 8.2. Transience as Liberation

In conventional art, the everlasting nature often creates a pressure for perfection. The ephemeral street artist, divested of this burden, is freed to experiment, innovate, and take risks. The inevitable dissolution of the artwork not only permits but encourages a continuous process of creation and recreation, sowing seeds of endless possibilities.

Each piece, unique in the moment, sparks public intrigue and invites shared experiences. The viewers, aware of the fleeting nature of these works, are urged to live in the here and now, capturing within them the transient beauty before it's washed away.

## 8.3. Journeys Beyond Physicality

Even though these works are transitory in nature, they are not bound by their physical limitations. With the advent of digital technology, artists and admirers alike can capture the artwork in a myriad of environments: under the radiant glow of the newly risen sun, in the harsh midday blues, or embraced by the crimson hues of the twilight.

Photographs, videos, and social media posts grant these transient masterpieces a form of digital immortality. The ephemeral art leaves the confinement of its geographical location, journeying to a world of screens on the other side of the globe, thus extending the reach and influence of the artist radically.

## 8.4. Brave New Voices

By challenging the traditional imperatives of durability, ephemeral street artists also defy societal norms and hierarchies. This mode of expression encompasses a broad palette of voices, often amplifying those that go unheard in mainstream society. These artists, relegated to the periphery, utilize the chemistry between expiration and creation to comment on various social issues.

# 8.5. The Tale of the Ephemeral Masterpieces

For the ephemeral artist, each art is a performance, a novel, a song sung for a fleeting second. This chapter unfolds the untold stories of such artists and their ephemeral masterpieces which, although washed away in the physical form, are eternally imprinted in the annals of urban memory.

In conclusion, through the impermanent, emotionally charged strokes of spray cans, rain-activated paints, and unconventional materials, ephemeral street artists capture and reflect the rhythm of urban metamorphosis, allowing the viewer to experience, however briefly, a glimpse into the ever-changing narratives that build our urban societies.

While these artworks may vanish – washed away by rain, faded by sunlight, or overridden by urban development – they leave behind potent reminders of the capacity of humans to share and engage in experiences with profound connectivity. Their presence may be fleeting, but in our consciousness, they are never truly forgotten. In reminding us that nothing lasts forever, ephemeral street art ingeniously infuses our daily urban experience with a profound sense of life's fleeting beauty.

# Chapter 9. When Nightmares Walk: The Intriguing World of Dark Street Art

Who can deny the allure of the shadows? They mesmerize, draw us with their impenetrable mystery, inviting exploration. Akin to this enigma is the realm of dark street art, an intriguing dimension where nightmares take flight, their noir feathers inked onto the insomnia of city walls and alleyway canvas. Vivid, poignant, often unsettling, this audacious genre provides a mesmerizing examination of society's underbelly, unveiling facets of our collective unconsciousness commonly shrouded in apprehension and secrecy.

## 9.1. The Alchemy of the Shadows: An Introduction

A world, as distant from the prudish daylight as darkness is from light itself, nightstreet art is a cathedral of the strange and the unconventional. Their alchemists, the artists, transform mundane blank walls into a theater of the unsettling, morphing the cityscape into a sprawling crypt of horrors and attractions.

Instrumental in revealing esteeming tales of human angst, dark street art is a catacomb of subliminal signifiers rife with symbolism. Their language, tenebrous and unfathomable, strikingly challenges our perception of aesthetic beauty and the unraveling of societal norms.

## 9.2. Monochrome Manifestos and Splashes of Vermilion: Form and Colors

Detaching from the kaleidoscopic extravagance of its customary counterparts, dark street art surrenders to the chastity of monochrome with occasional, dramatic accents of red. The stark, black ink that festoons across the emptiness is eerily consistent with the element of darkness they depict, while the evocative expression of red, often symbolizing violence or passion, accentuates the depth of an image's narrative. Be it a skeletal hand reaching for an anatomical heart, or a creature from an unbounded nightmare, the infusion of colors remains minimalistic, intentional, and impactful.

## 9.3. The Theater of Street Walls: Motifs and Symbols

The artists of the night are not ghoulish beings, rather our narrators of grand, mystifying tales. Utilizing wall as their canvas, they imprint recurring motifs ripe with symbolism, their images ensnared in storytelling's grand web. Notably, these nocturnal murals frequently showcase haunting distortions of human figures, monstrous entities, eerie biomorphic forms, and intricately twisted typographies - each bearing stories intricately tied into human emotions, socio-political innuendos, and cultural critiques.

Each figure, twisted or metamorphosed, interprets a reality difficult to digest. A distorted, amputated humanoid signals towards loss and tragedy, whilst a grinning beast draws attention to the lurking barbarousness within societal order. Symbols are stark, unnerving, yet wholly open to individual interpretation.

# 9.4. Artists of the Underworld: Prominent Figures

There remains no paucity of talent within this underworld of artistic expression. Artists such as Banksy, Blek le Rat, and the anonymous horror-artist Nychos, grace the night with stunning displays of their discerning proficiency. Banksy's 'Grim Reaper' rendered on a wall in a parking lot, or a dissected rabbit by Nychos - each of these art pieces signify moments of macabre woven into the urban fabric. These creators harness the power of night's landscape, drawing life from its spectral playground.

# 9.5. Shadowy Narratives: Storytelling through Dark Street Art

Each image, a poignant poem inked in the cobweb of the night, holds a mirror to society's face, distressing yet difficult to turn away from. Compelling narratives lie embedded under grotesque figures, staring into the void of the spectator's comprehension. Protest against war, commentary on capitalism, and portrayal of mortality are just a few of the numerous facets explored through this form of vivid artistic expression.

Adhering to their rebellious roots, these dark duchies of street art provide the canvas for artists to emblazon their nightmares publicly. They become the voice of the unheard, manifesting the silent woes that reverberate in their minds, imposed by a society radiating splintering dissonance in ideas of righteousness and freedom.

In conclusion, dark street art is not merely a form of nonconformist creative expression but an emerald portal into the furthest recesses of the human psyche. Brittle boundaries between dreams and reality blur in this shadowy realm. It is an ode to the uncanny tales of life, etched in the whispers of the urban wilderness. It reminds us that art is an ever-evolving beast, one that is tethered to the world's shifting ecosystems, living and breathing through the canvas of our shared experiences. Without fear, the artists of the night continue to evoke intrigue and pay homage to the enduring wonder of the human condition.

# Chapter 10. In Their Words: Interviews with Unconventional Street Artists

First off, we dive right into the world of unconventional graffiti with an in-depth interview with the notorious street artist, Dusk. Known for his signature sketches which often present captivating scenes of urban jungle life, Dusk challenges our understanding of graffiti, transforming ordinary cityscapes with his bold lines, intricate details, and complex symbols.

## 10.1. Dusk: The Urban Jungle Whisperer

*Interviewer*: "Dusk, your works are impossible to miss - popping with life, etching a breath of wilderness into concrete city landscapes. What inspired you to bring the jungle to the city through your art?"

*Dusk*: "Well, it's an irony I've come to embrace - that while we're in the midst of extreme urbanization, there's still a primal call of the wild within us. This juxtaposition of urban life and wildlife in my art, it's an echo of that call, a reminder of our natural roots."

In a similarly defiant artistic spirit, our next street artist, Echo, uses graffiti to articulate her critiques of modern society. Her workspace, the city streets, bear witness to her evocative messages.

## 10.2. Echo: Reflecting Society in Spray Paint

*Interviewer*: "Echo, your works speak volumes about socio-political issues. When did you decide to engrave these deep societal concerns onto the streets through graffiti?"

*Echo*: "Art has always been a vehicle for self-expression and commentary. I realized that the streets, which everyone traverses, are the perfect platform to highlight these issues. The immediacy of graffiti also adds to the urgency of these social discussions."

Moving from substantive commentary to abstract storytelling, meet Stardust, an artist whose graffiti spins enticing tales from other worlds.

# 10.3. Stardust: Galactic Graffiti Poet

*Interviewer*: "Stardust, your graffiti is an adventure into the unknown, a dive into galaxies often only explored through literature. Why did you decide to narrate these celestial stories through your work?"

*Stardust*: "I've always been a stargazer. My imagination, ignited by the night sky, wander to distant galaxies and intriguing civilizations. Graffiti allows me to materialize these dreams, sparking curiosity and wonder in others."

Lastly, we turn our attention to another equally fascinating entity in the street art circuit - Phantasma, whose works ambitiously toe the line between reality and fantasy.

# 10.4. Phantasma: The Dream Weaver

*Interviewer*: "Phantasma, your work finds a delicate balance between the real and the unreal with scenes that seem plucked directly from dreams. What inspired your surreal interpretations?"

*Phantasma*: "Dreams render the illogical logical, the impossible feasible and the invisible visible. This whimsical quality fascinates me. Through my graffiti, I facilitate viewers to experience a similar blurring of reality and illusion."

Each of these artists, in expressing their unique aims and inspirations, open a window into the broader world of unconventional street art. Their vibrant compositions and heartfelt offerings push the boundaries of traditional conception of art, making the streets a living, breathing gallery on which their stories unfold and evolve. Whether it is Dusk's call of the wild, Echo's social commentaries, Stardust's celestial adventures, or Phantasma's dreamscapes, their art, in thoughtfully coloring the uncared corners, serves as an eloquent testament to the inner lives of our cities.

This chapter provides an eye-opening insight into the minds of unconventional street artists. The interviews, unfolding a rich variety of themes and techniques, are a testament to the multitudinous mysteries the walls have to offer, inviting us to appreciate the beauty and stories that lie within urban spaces, and inspiring a new generation to continue painting such compelling narratives. This, indeed, is the stranger side of street art.

# Chapter 11. From Grit to Gallery: The Transmutation of Street Art

Red brick walls, abandoned buildings, and desolate subway stations form the unlikely provenance of a culture now loudly echoing across the polished hallways of galleries and museums worldwide. A culture as misunderstood as it is controversial - street art.

Street art, once the seat of rebellion, has ripened into a respected art form, stirring up conversations in contemporary art scenes around the globe. Its metamorphosis from grit to gallery, fraught with hurdles and imbued with resilience, serves as testimony to the transformative power of artistic expression.

## 11.1. The Humble Beginnings

The dawn of street art coincides with the emergence of hip hop in the 1970s in New York City. While tracks, turntables, and microphones birthed a new sound, graffiti artists, synonymous with this counter-culture, wielded spray cans as their voice. The walls were their canvas, calling out tales of social disparities, political unrest, and the mundane rhythms of life in the Bronx.

The scene was raw. Talent was plentiful, but the recognition was scant, coming largely from within the community. Graffiti artist Lee Quiñones exhales an often forgotten reality, "You'd finish a piece, admire it, take a picture, and then it was gone, melting into the city." This 'here today, gone tomorrow' essence was part of the game; the artists craved not permanence, but expression.

# 11.2. A Cultural Shift

As the 80s rolled around, street art morphed into a symbol of corruption and lawlessness, closely tethered to crime-filled neighborhoods. However, mindful observers began detaching the art from its environment, seeing it instead as a reflection of the societal unrest fostering it. Graffiti was consequently propelled from the realms of vandalism, stepping tentatively into the world of art.

In the early years, Jean-Michel Basquiat and Keith Haring, both renowned artists of their time and former graffiti writers, played instrumental roles in this transition. Their white-canvas works exhibited at swanky galleries were imbued with street art sensibilities, subtly implanting the graffiti aesthetic into the mainstream art consciousness.

# 11.3. Street Art Gets 'Banksied'

The new millennium ushered in the era of Banksy, a pseudonymous England-based artist whose satirical stencils thrummed with political and social commentary. Banksy's mystique, coupled with his audacious overnight displays, stirred public curiosity while spotlighting the visual potency of street art.

His pieces began fetching high prices at auction houses. "Girl with Balloon" famously sold for over a million dollars despite shredding itself at the moment of sale, a reaffirmation of Banksy's satirical critique of the art world. It was becoming abundantly clear - street art was no longer limited to the pavement; it had found itself a seat at the high table.

# 11.4. Contemporary Galleries and Street Art

Today, the walls of esteemed institutions and galleries worldwide reverberate with the echoes of the street. Exhibitions like "Beyond the Streets" or the Museum of Contemporary Art's groundbreaking "Art in the Streets" are more than mere collection showcases. They constitute an important shift, validating an art form birthed from urban grit, validating street art.

Admittedly, there is controversy. Critics argue that transitioning to galleries strips street art of its rawness, its essence. Others praise the shift, citing increased exposure and deserved acceptance for the artists. Despite the debates, it's undeniable that this shift has reframed the public perception, replacing the derision with admiration.

# 11.5. Beyond the Frame

As we unravel this evolution, it's essential to remember that galleries and museums are but one stage for street art. The transmutation of street art is not merely about a physical shift but about the perception and valuation. It is about understanding that the art form is malleable enough to thrive in a gritty alley and a gallery with an equal degree of authenticity and resonance.

From wall to canvas, from civil disobedience to rebellious acceptance, the journey of street art remains as unfettered and defiant as the artists who breathe life into this spiraling kaleidoscope of color, iconography, and social commentary. One thing's certain - as long as there are stories to tell, street art, in all its unusual splendor, will continue to evolve, breaking boundaries, challenging norms, and redefining itself constantly. The intriguing transmutation continues.

In closing, turn back to the immortal words of Banksy – "Art should comfort the disturbed and disturb the comfortable." Whether etched on a quiet corner wall or displayed in an esteemed gallery, this sentiment echoes in every stroke of street art, reaffirming its intention as a harbinger of dialogue, change, and revolution. So, here's to the storytellers of the streets, who've wreaked beautiful havoc in the art world. Their voices, now echoing beyond city blocks, continue to carry the spirit of street right into the core of galleries worldwide, an amalgam as vibrant, complex, and vital as the artistry it upholds.